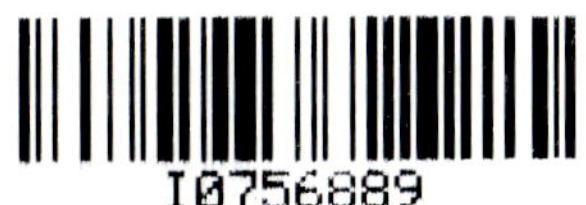

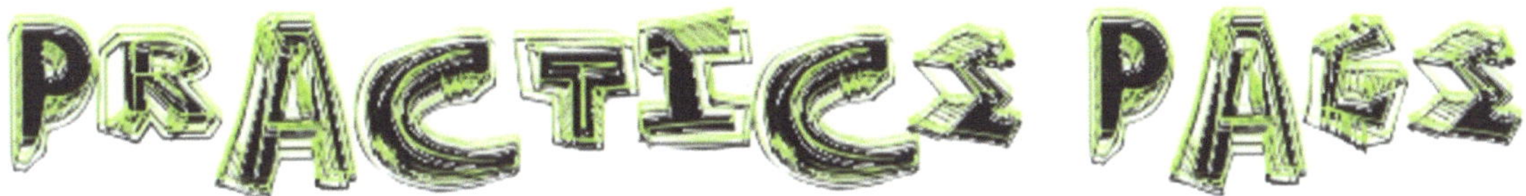

TEST YOUR COLORS HERE

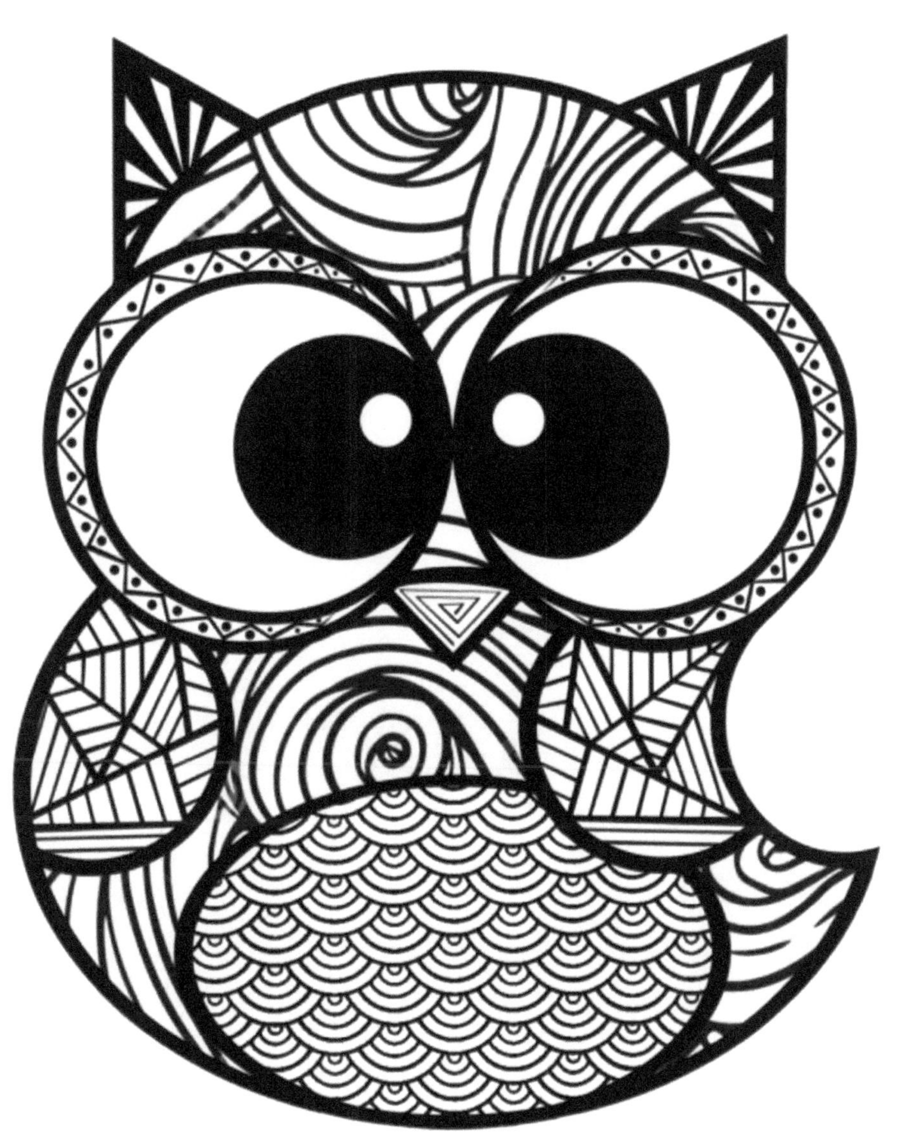

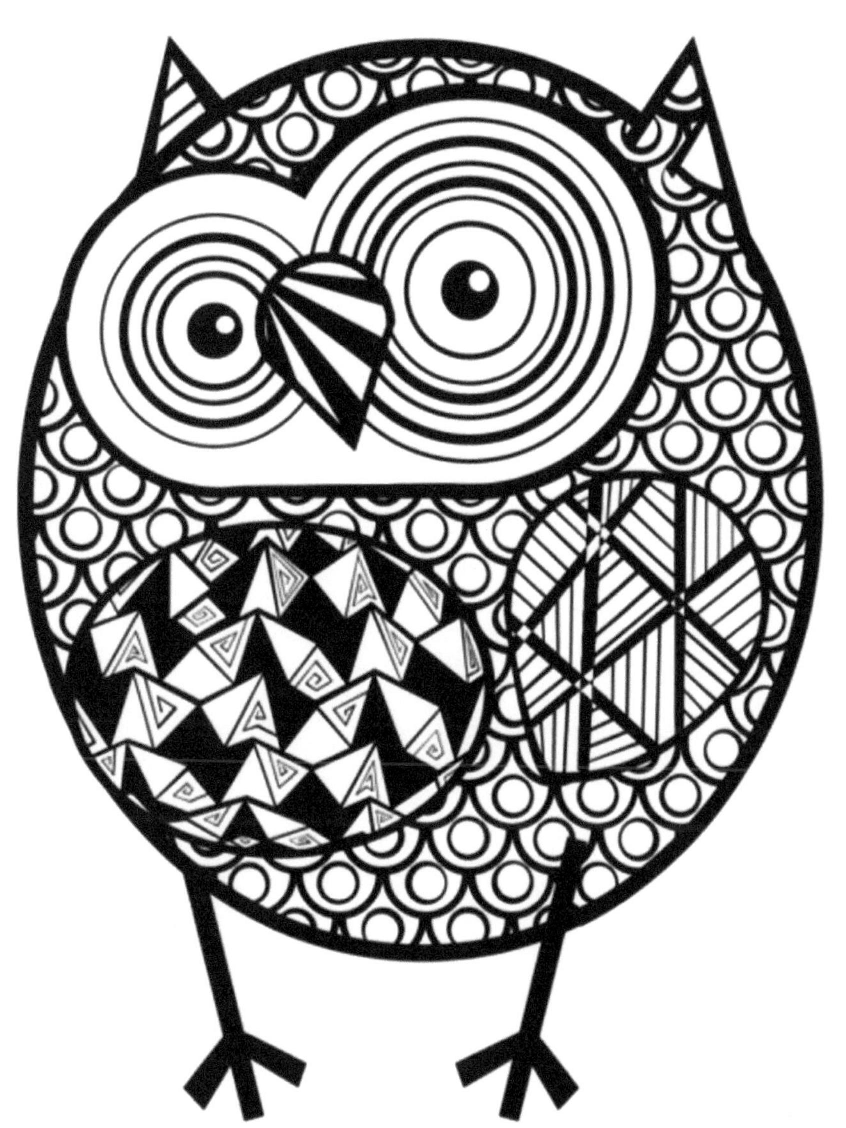

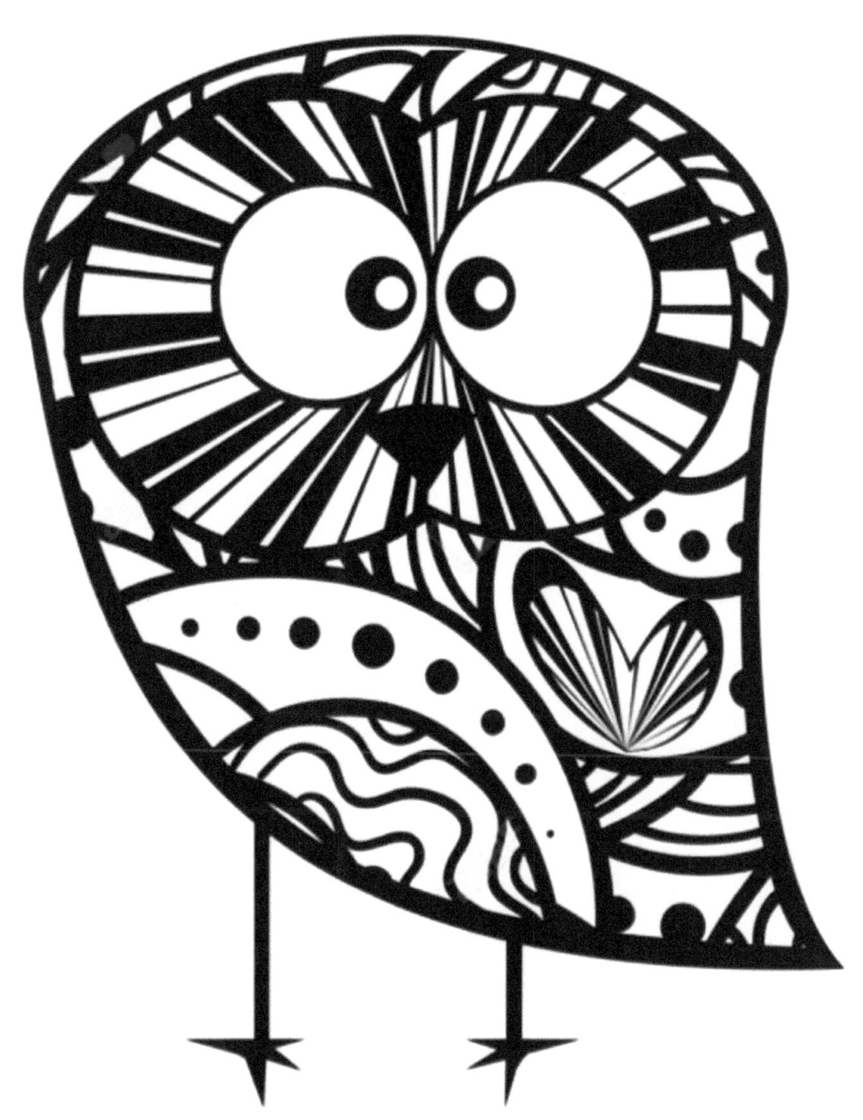

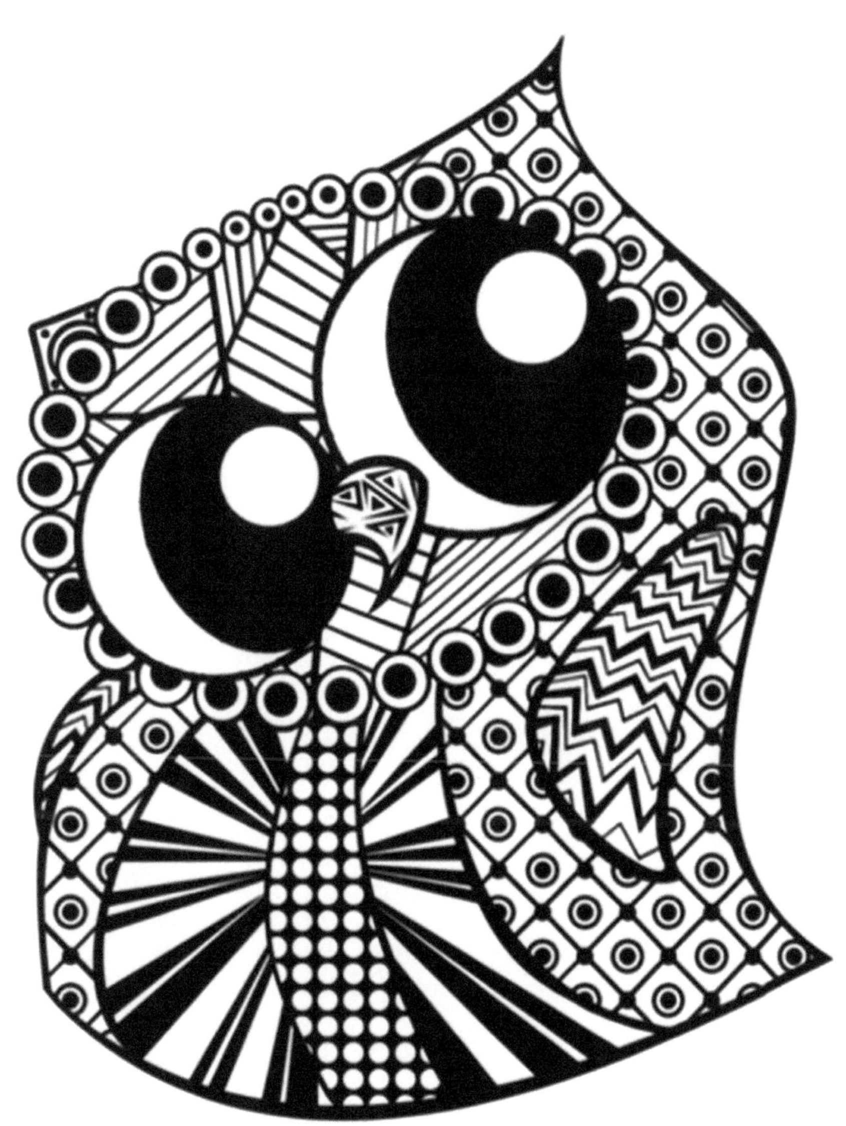

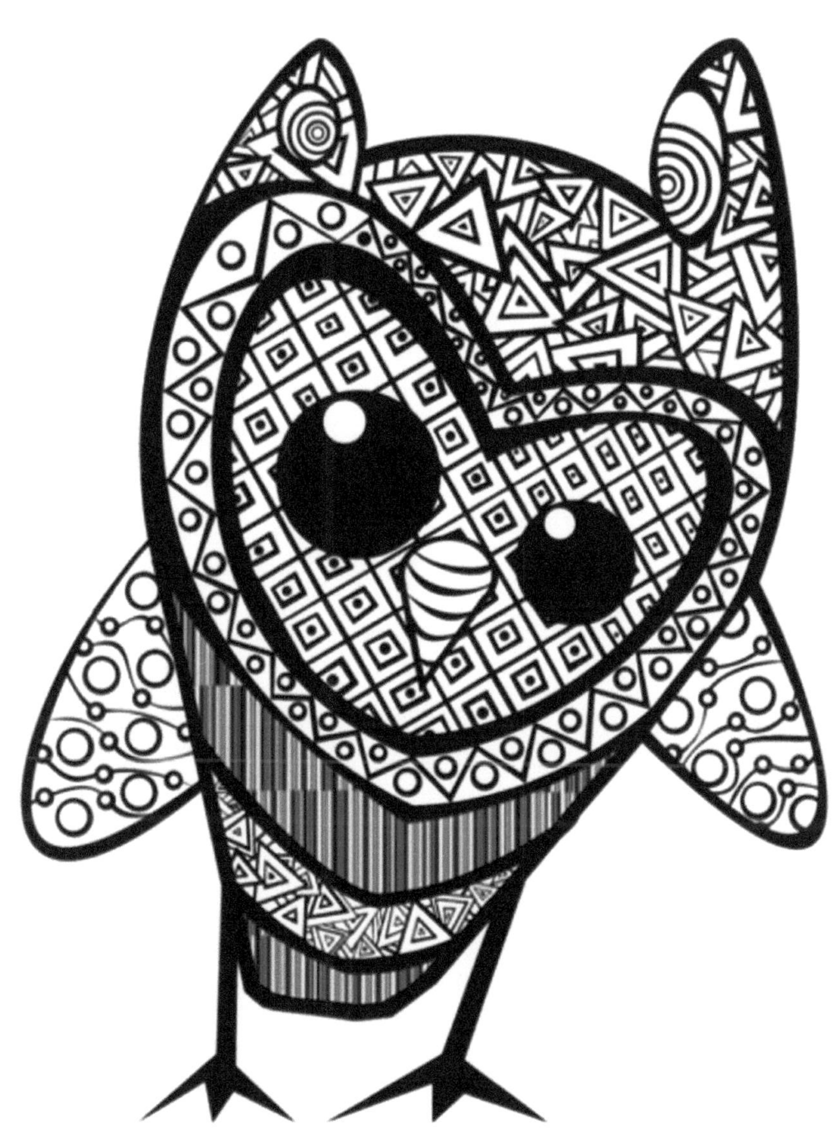

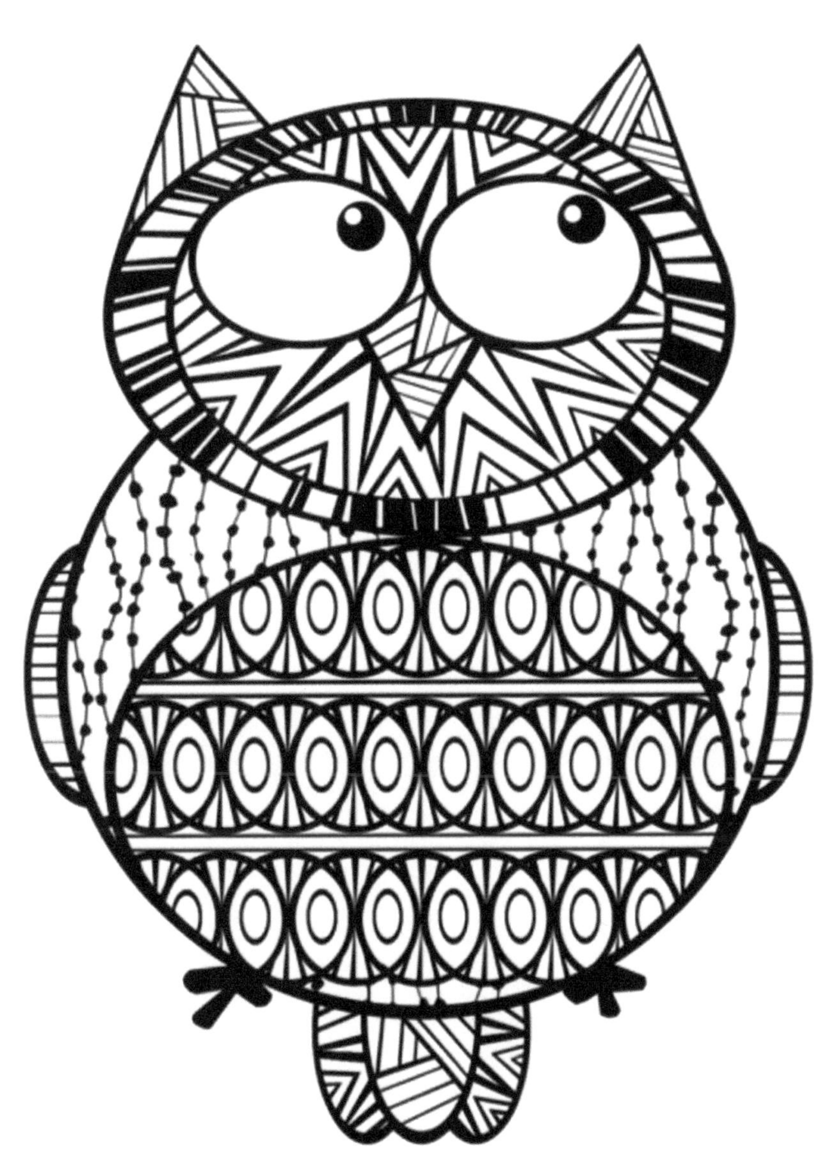

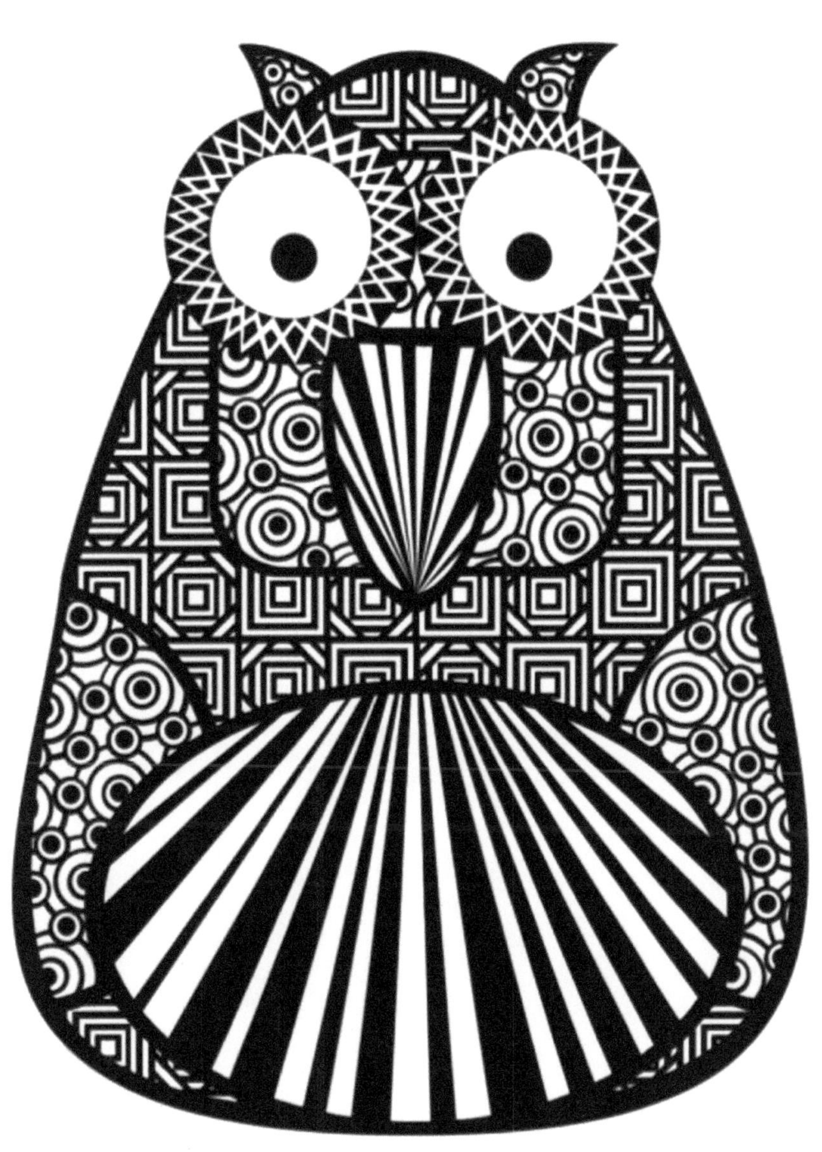

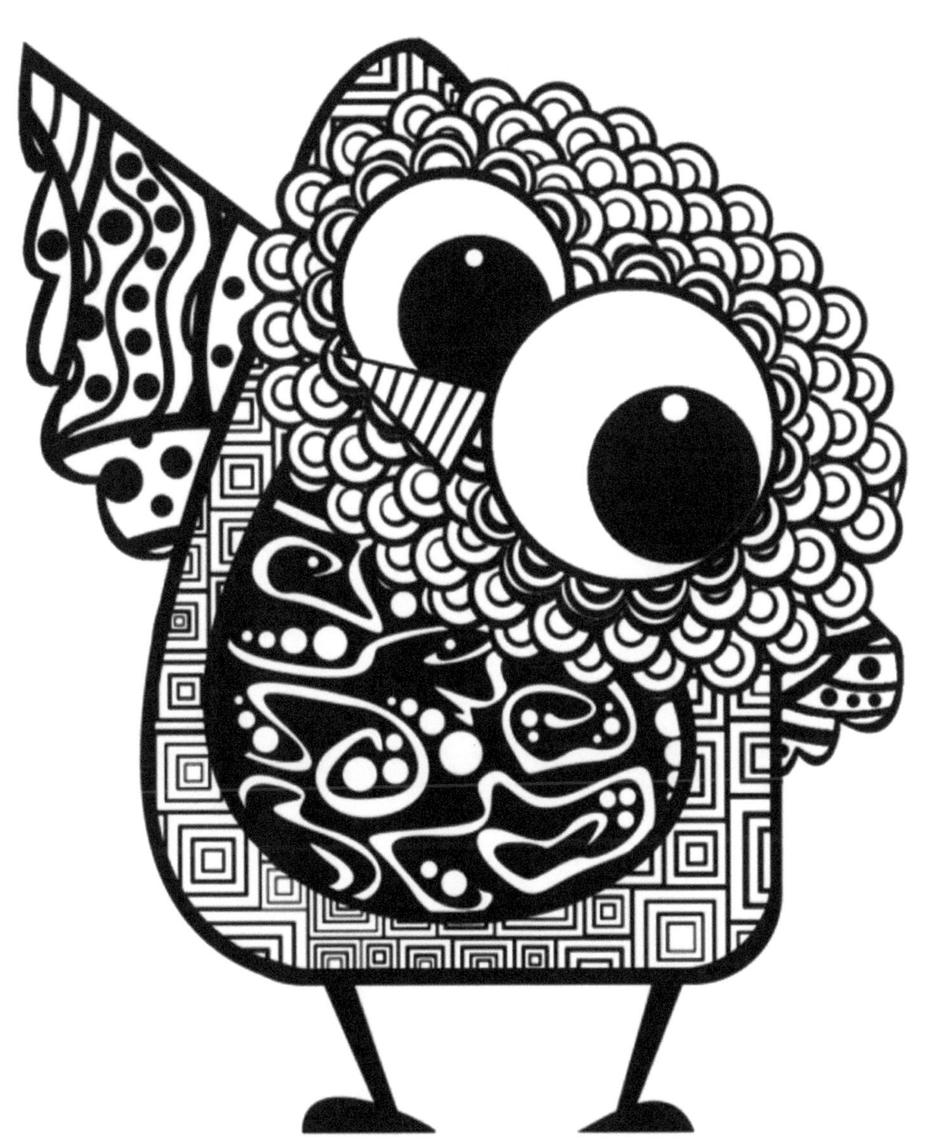

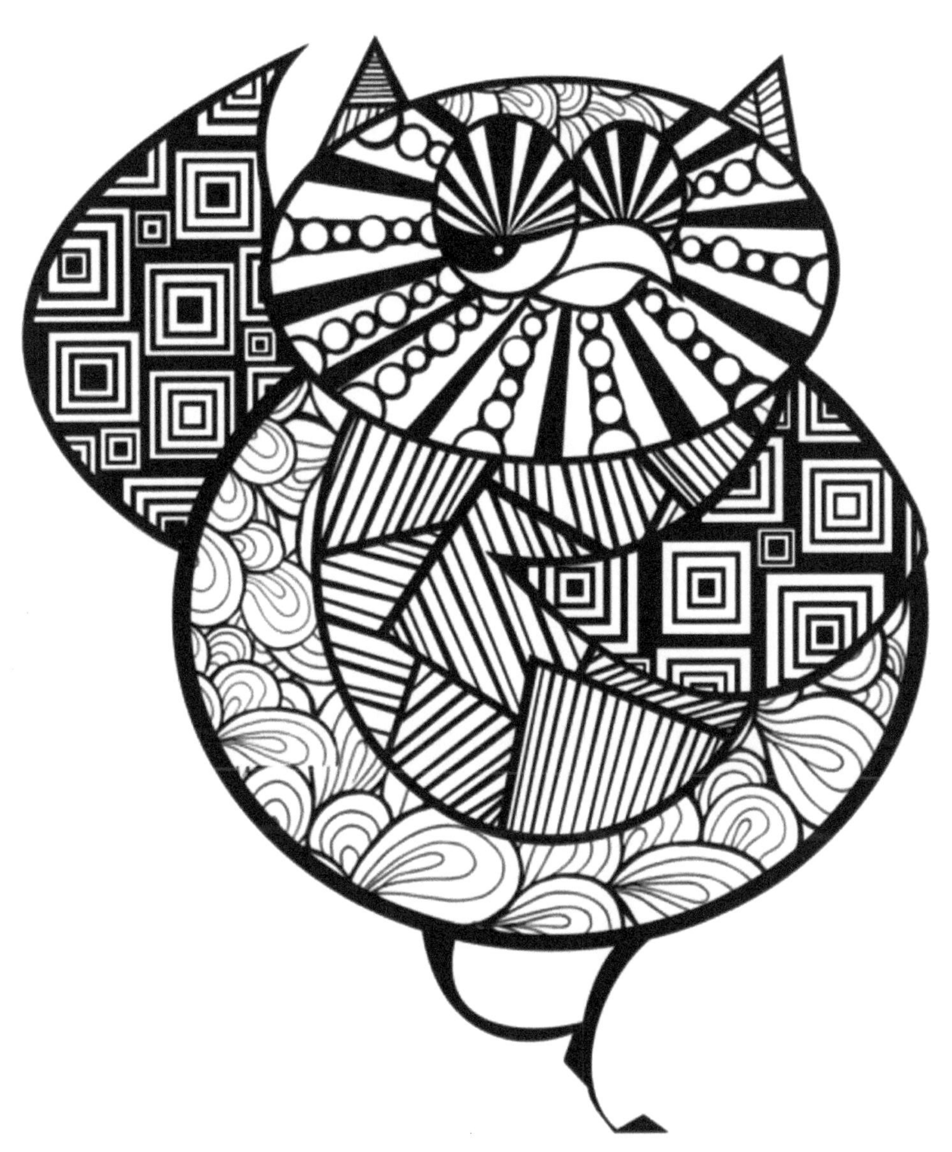

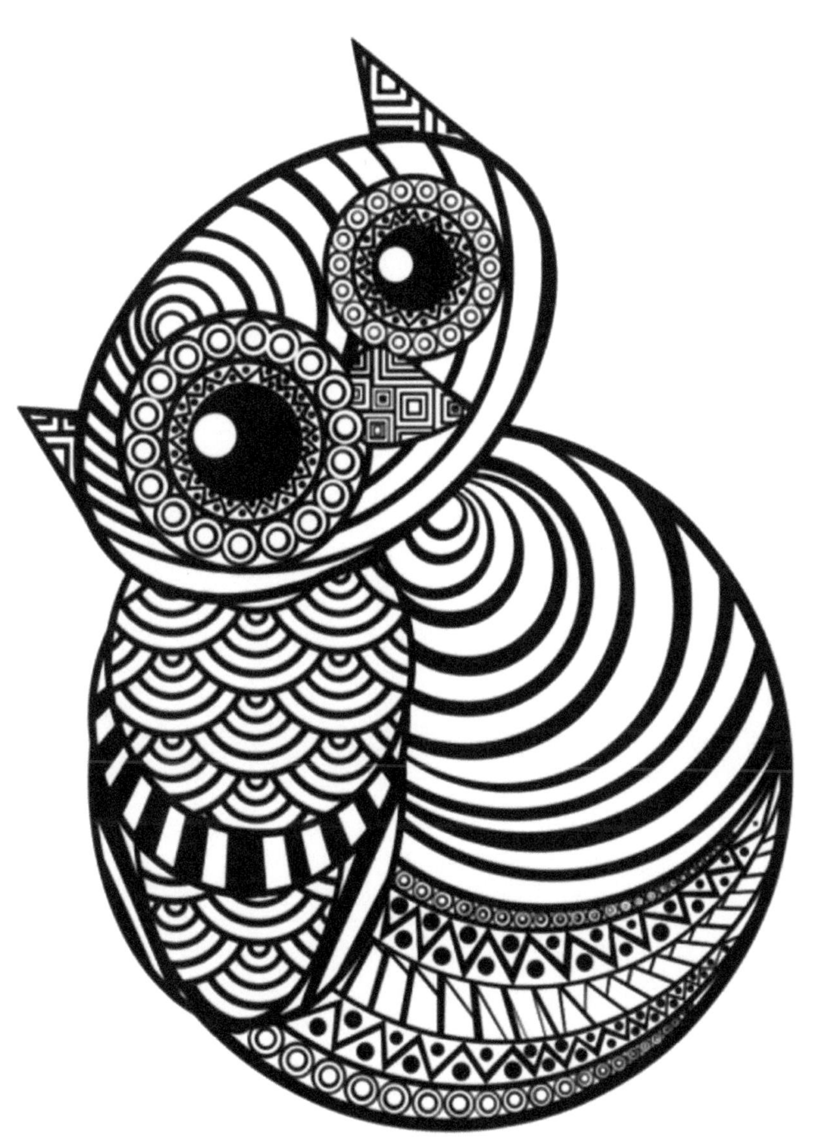

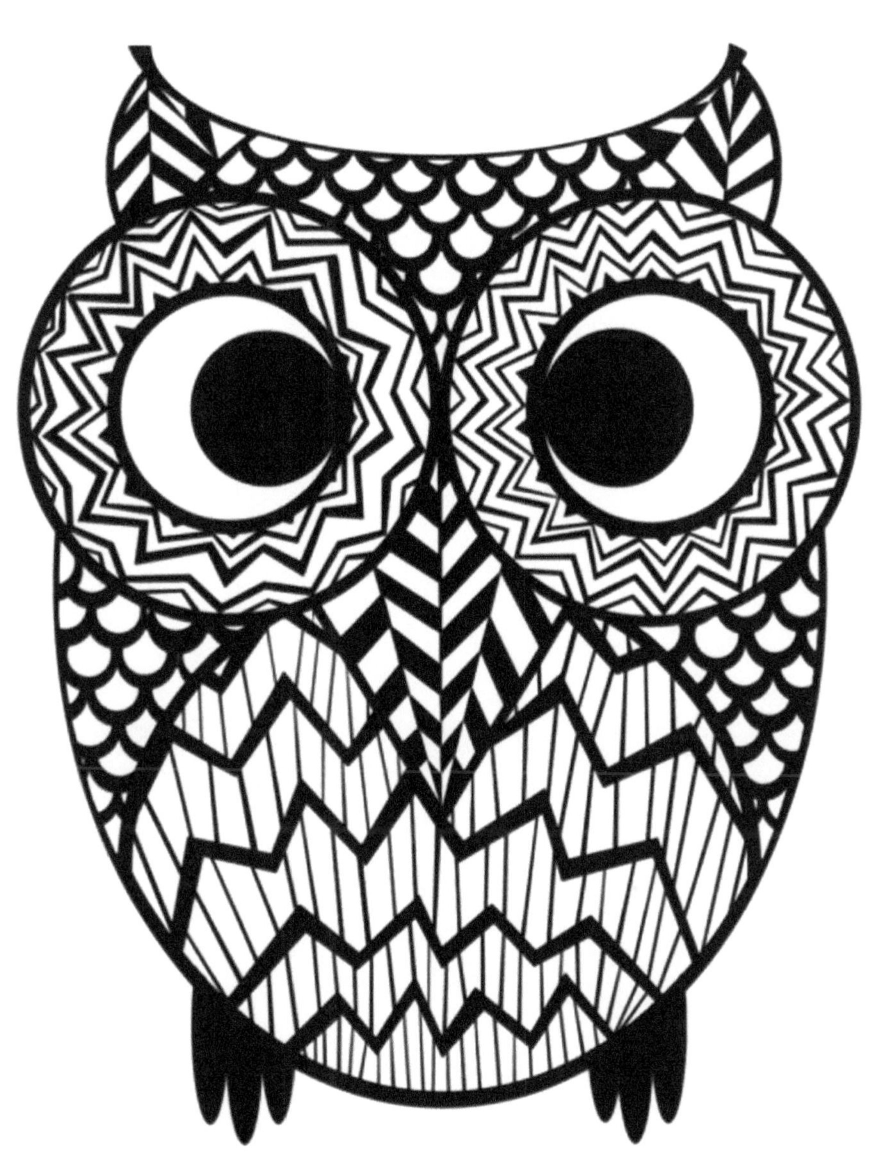

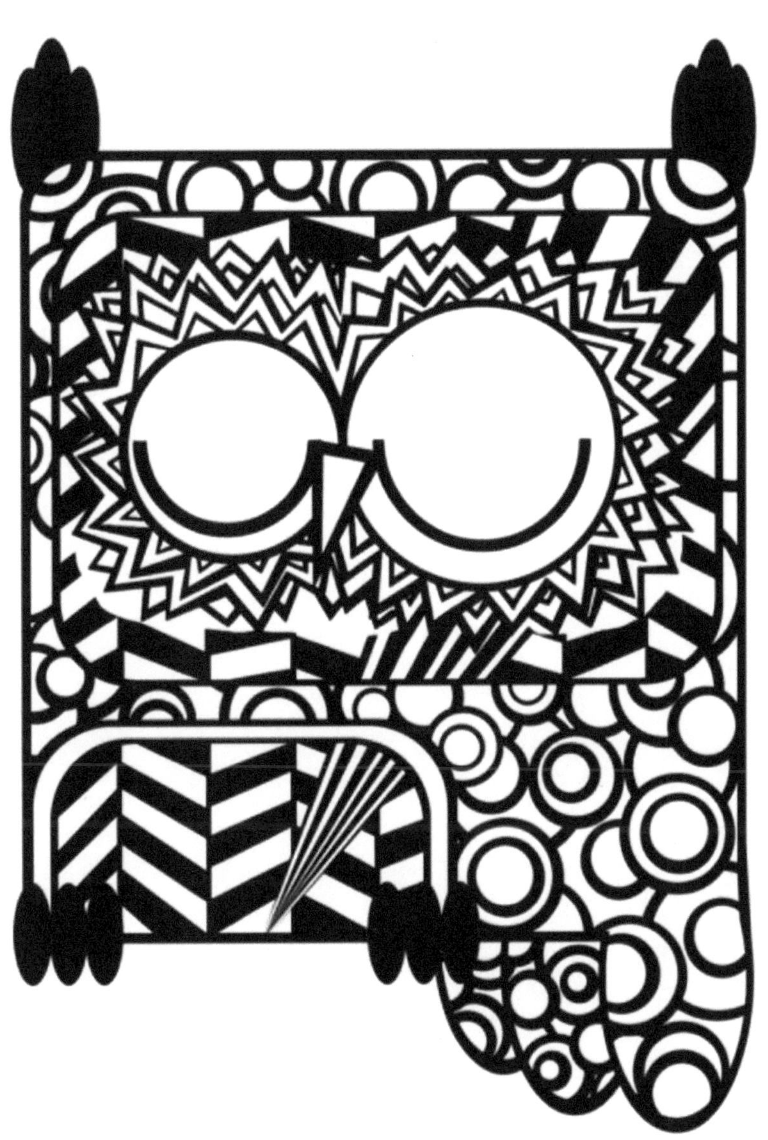

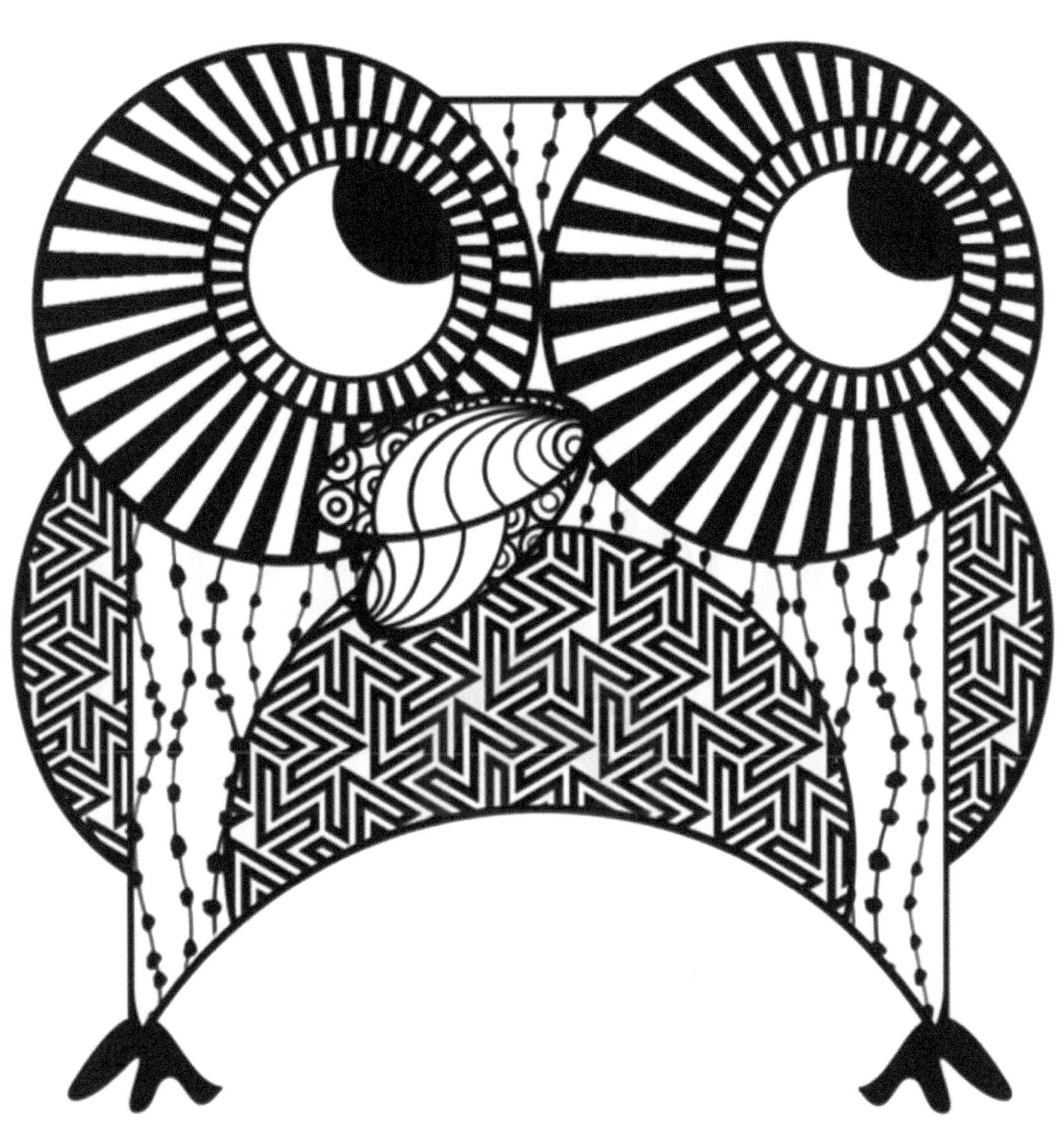

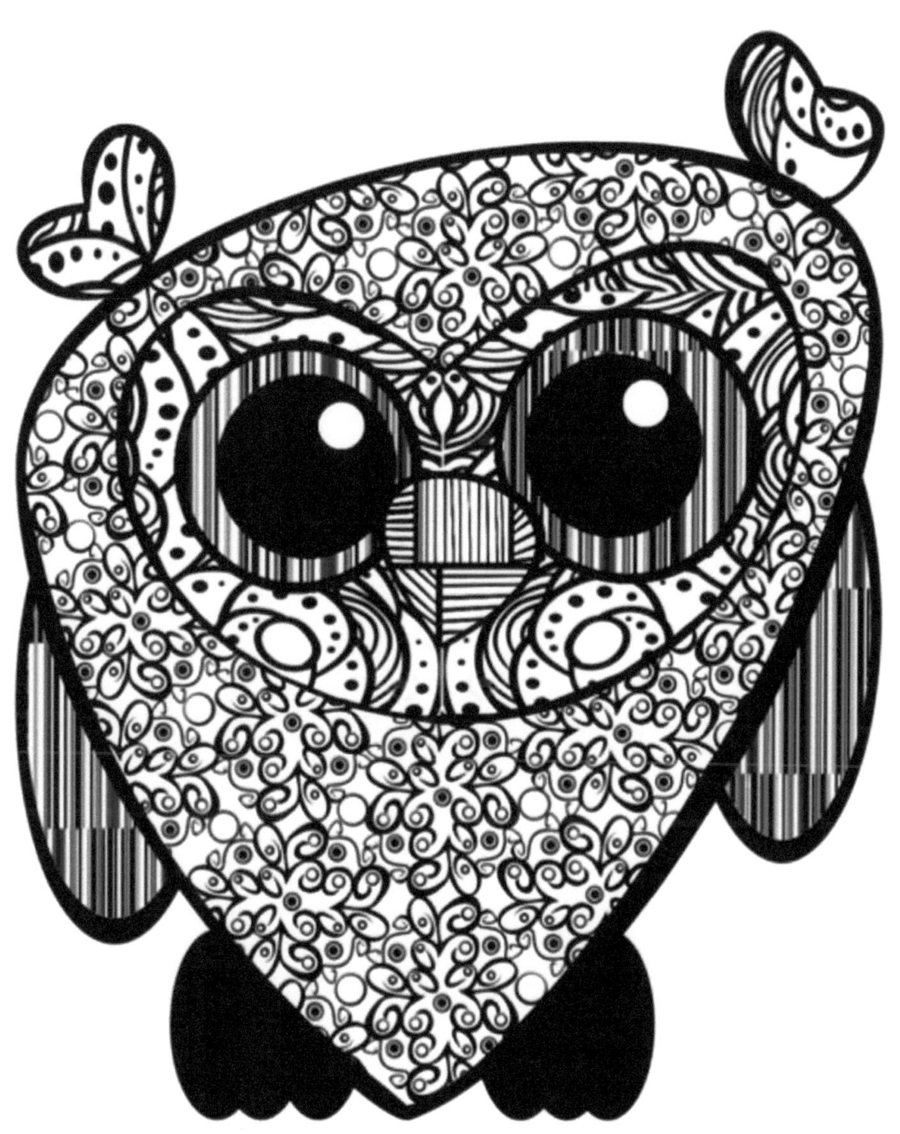

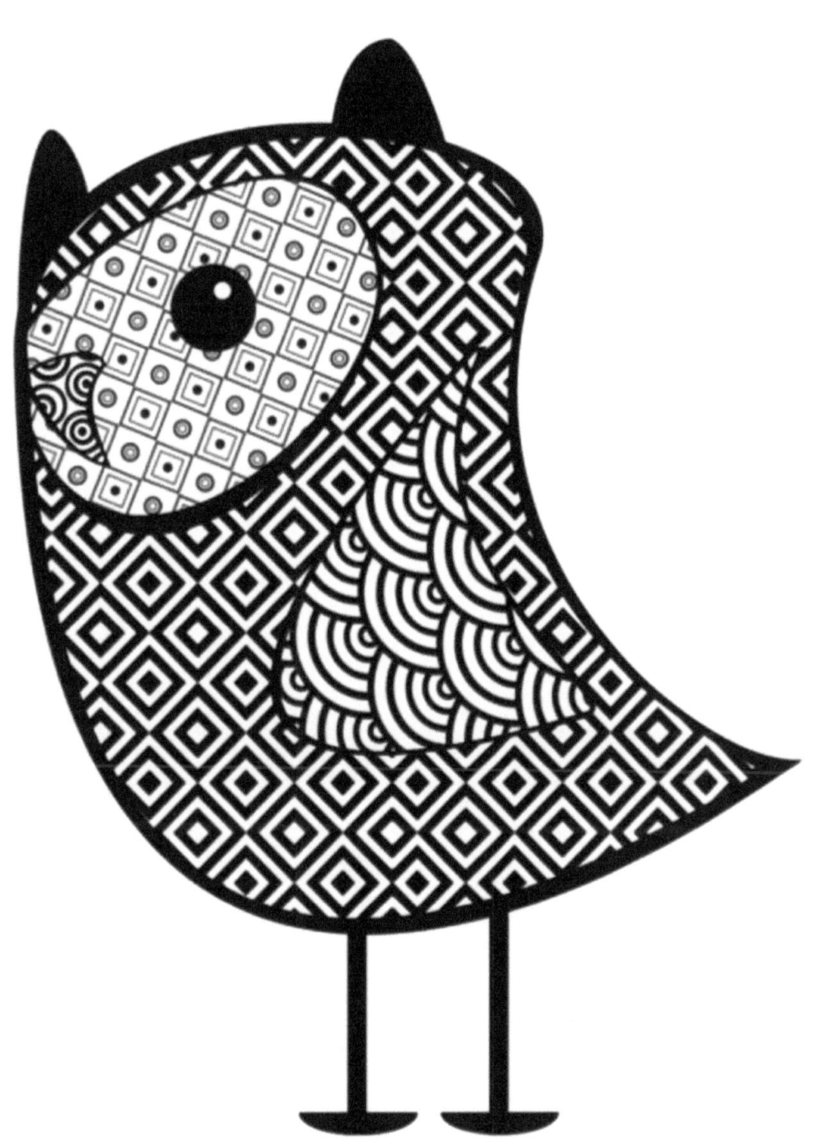

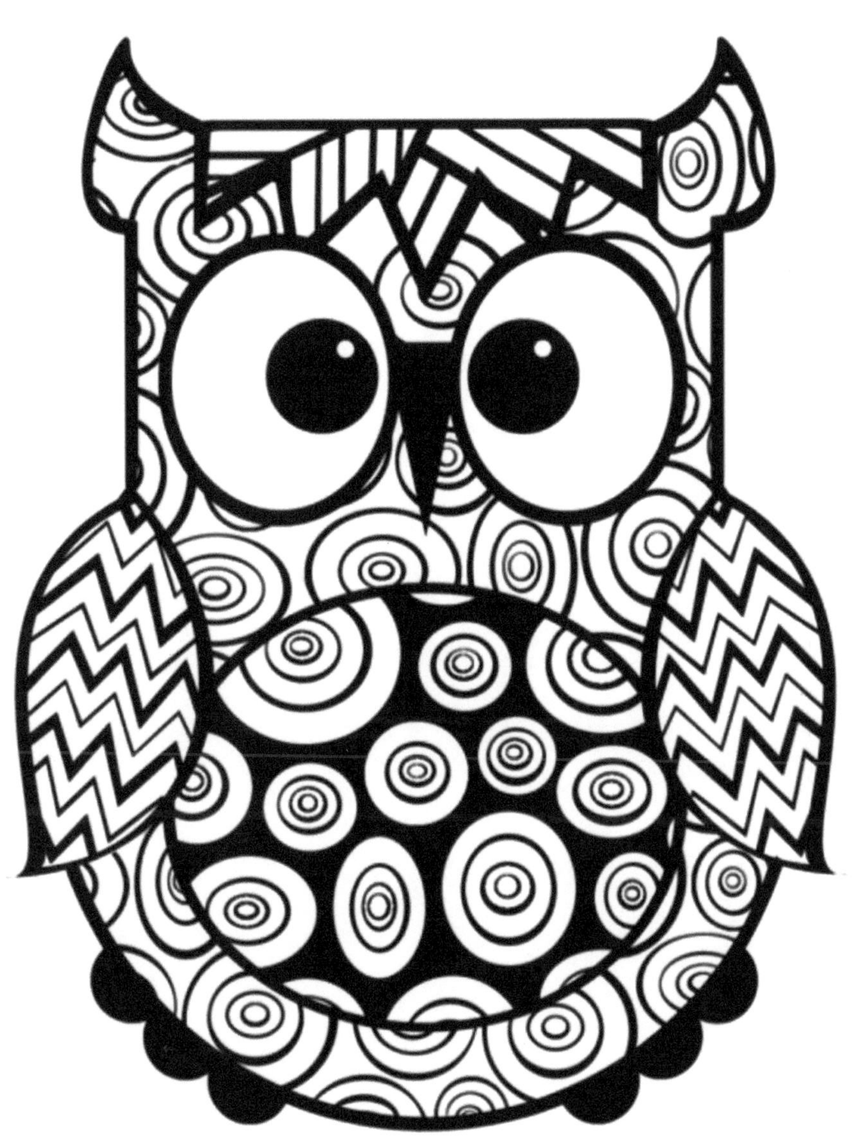

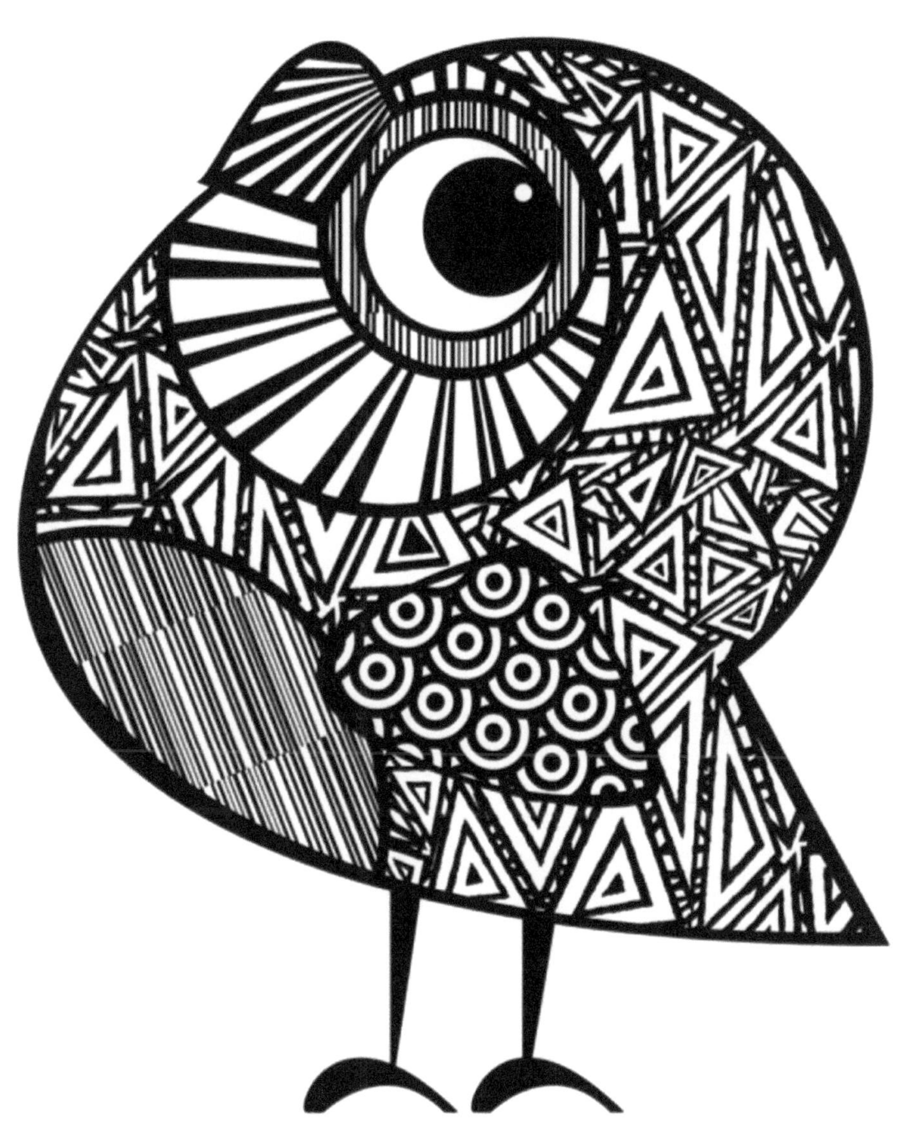

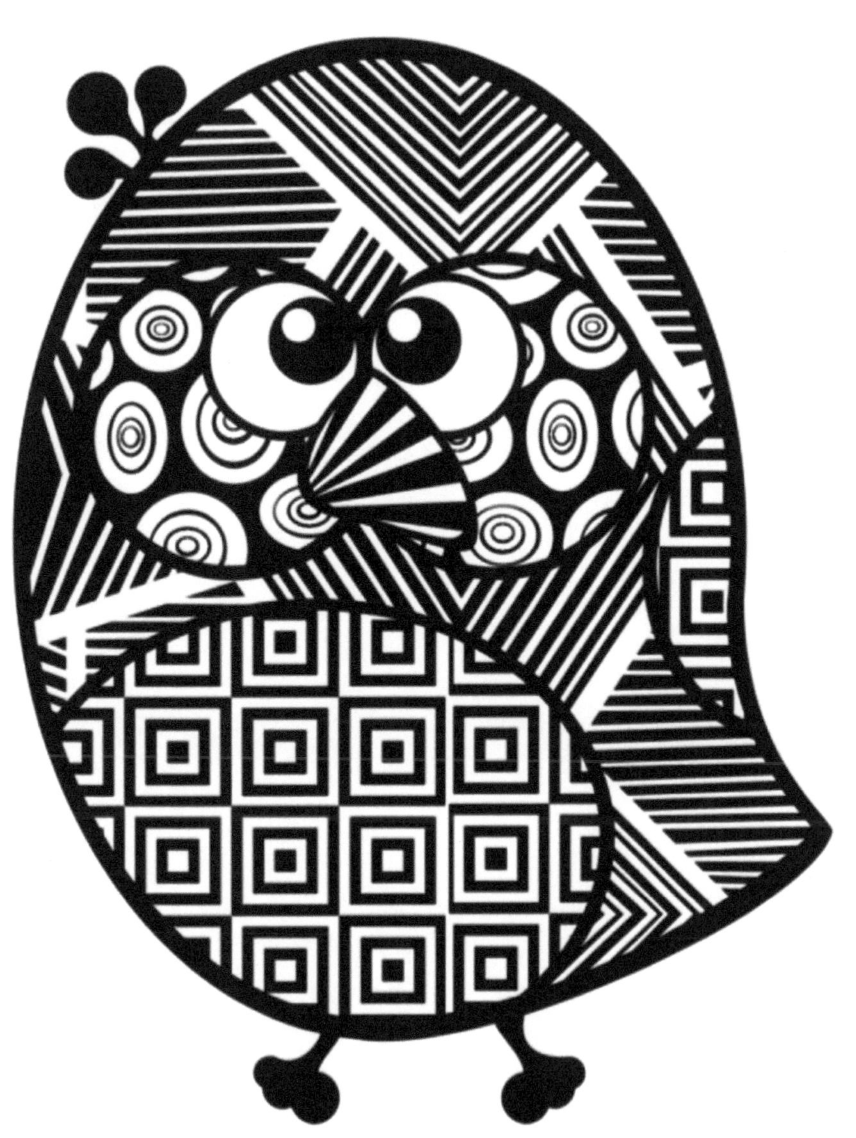

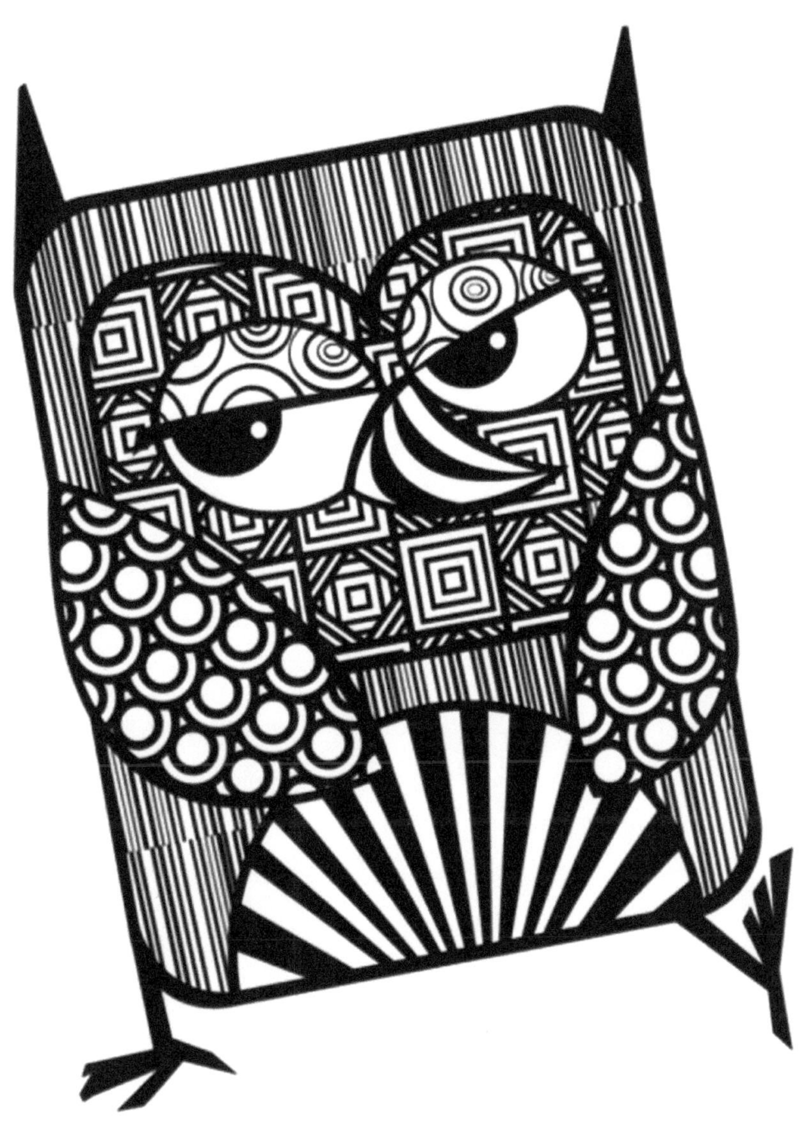

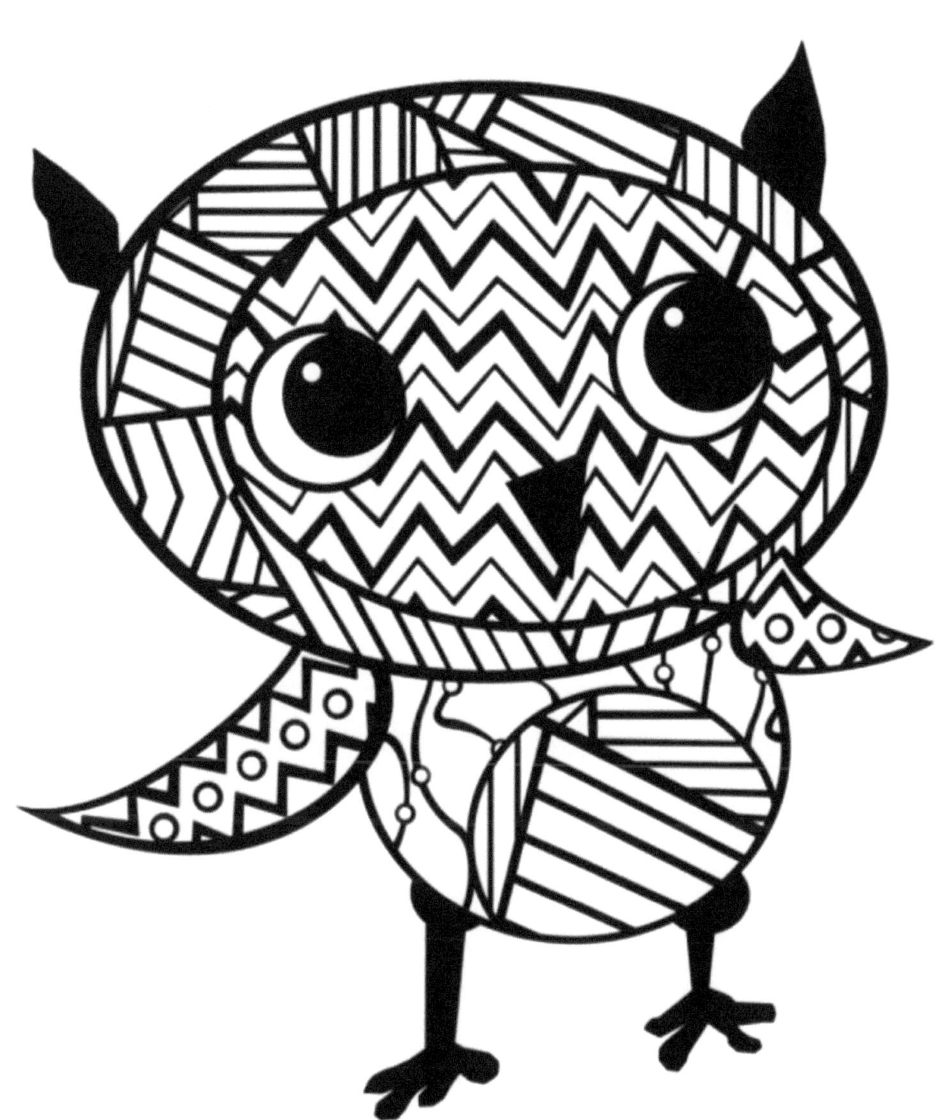

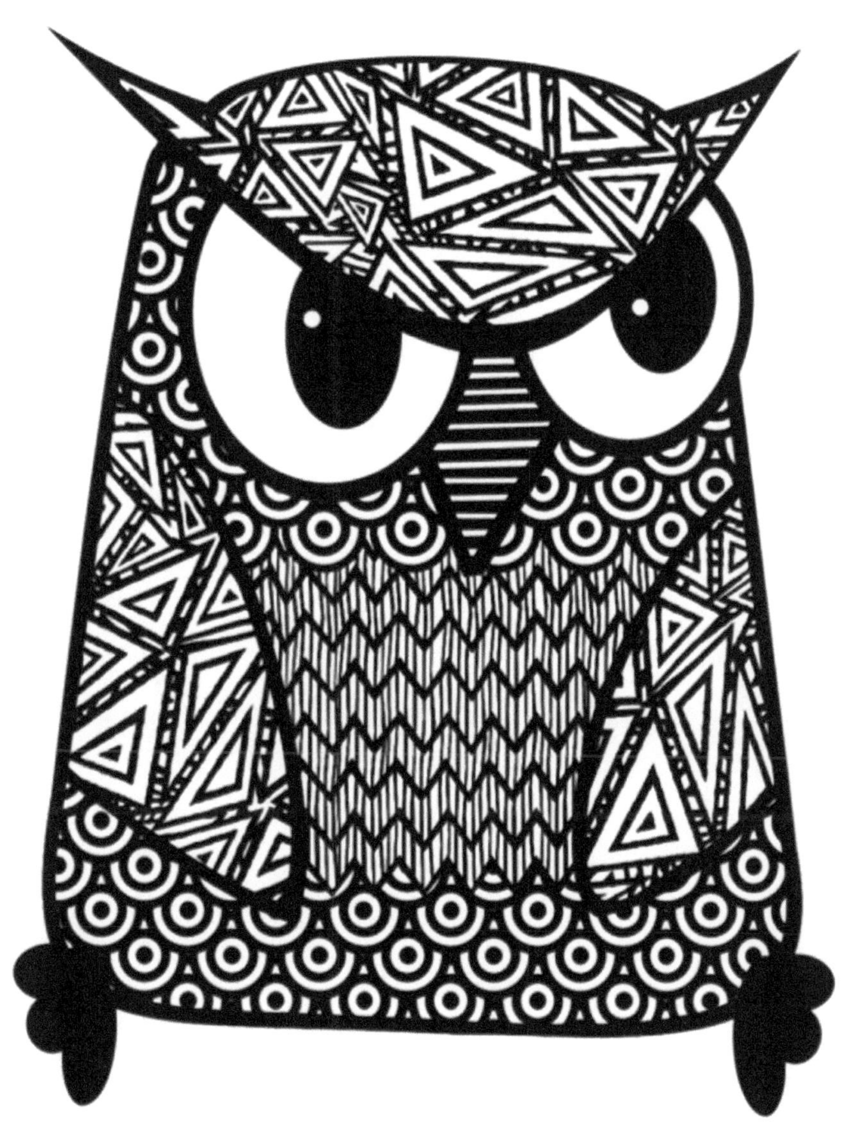

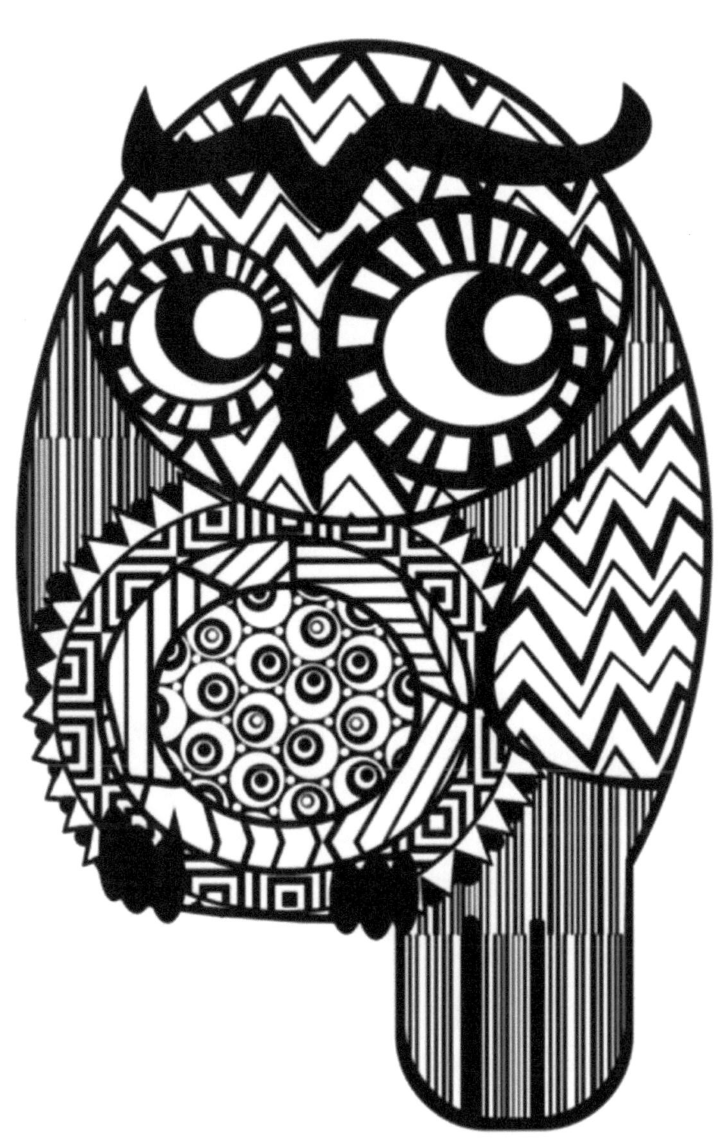

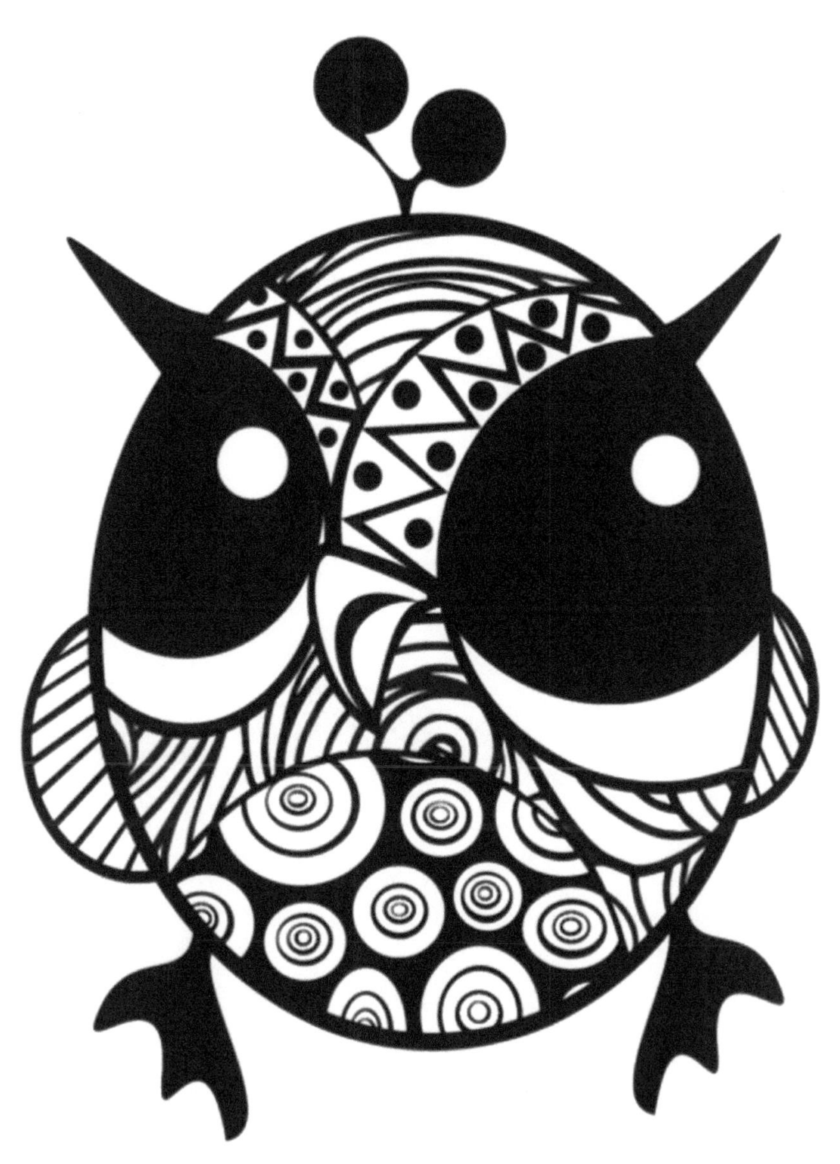

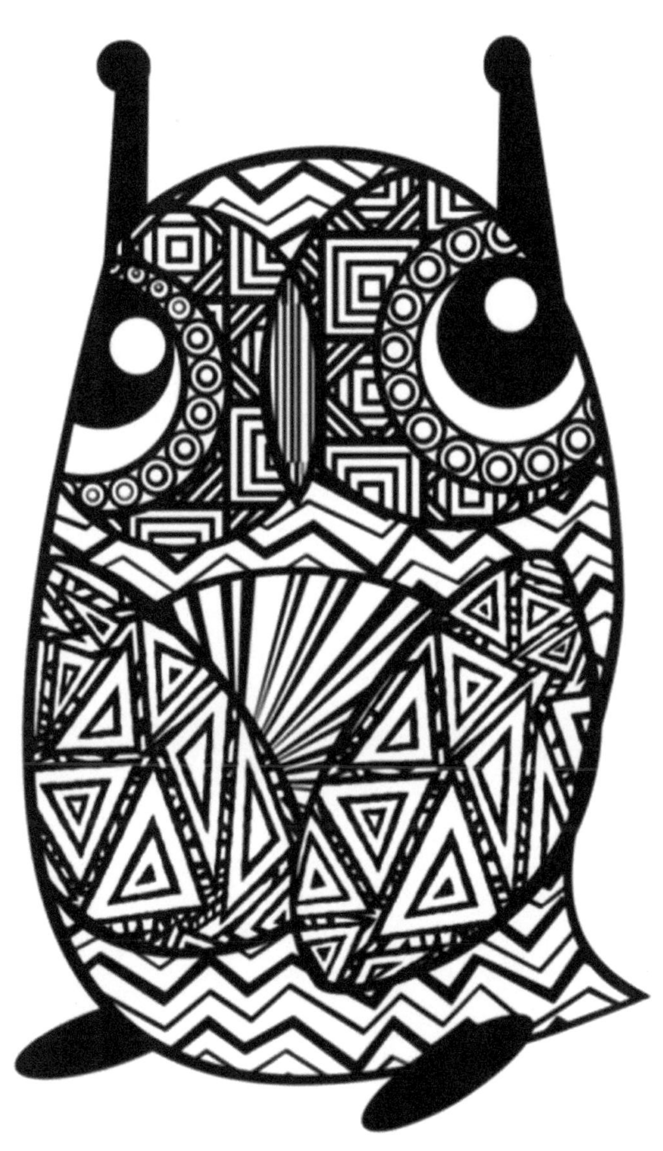

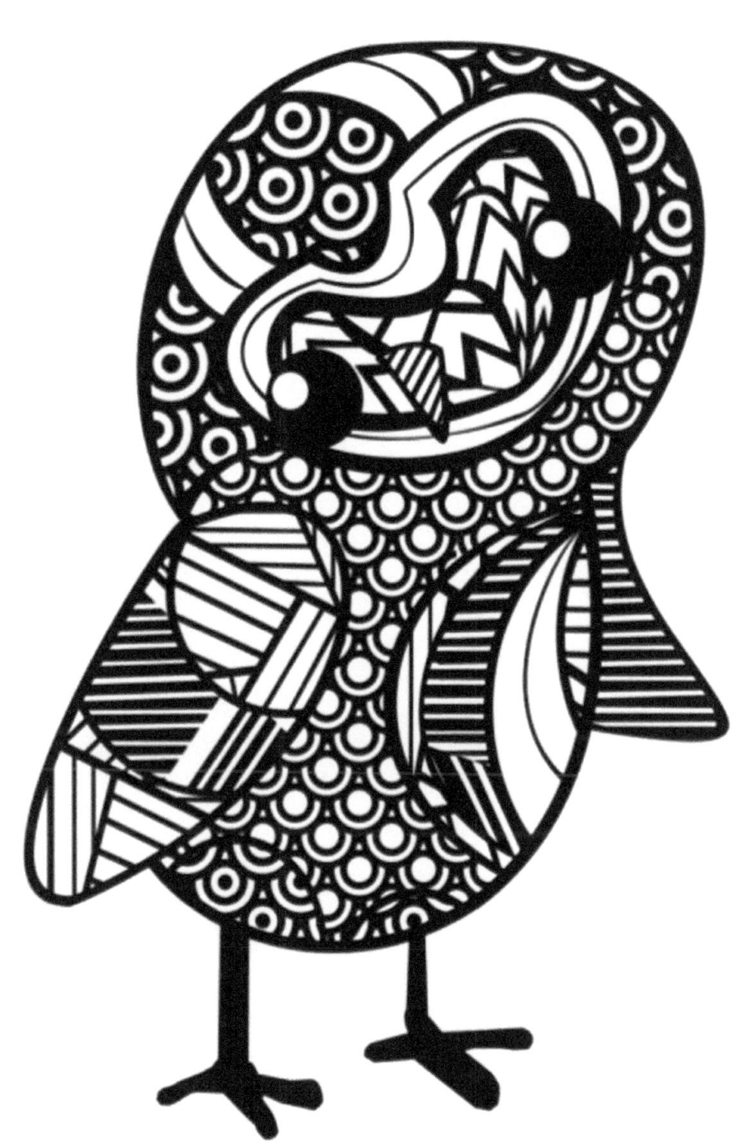

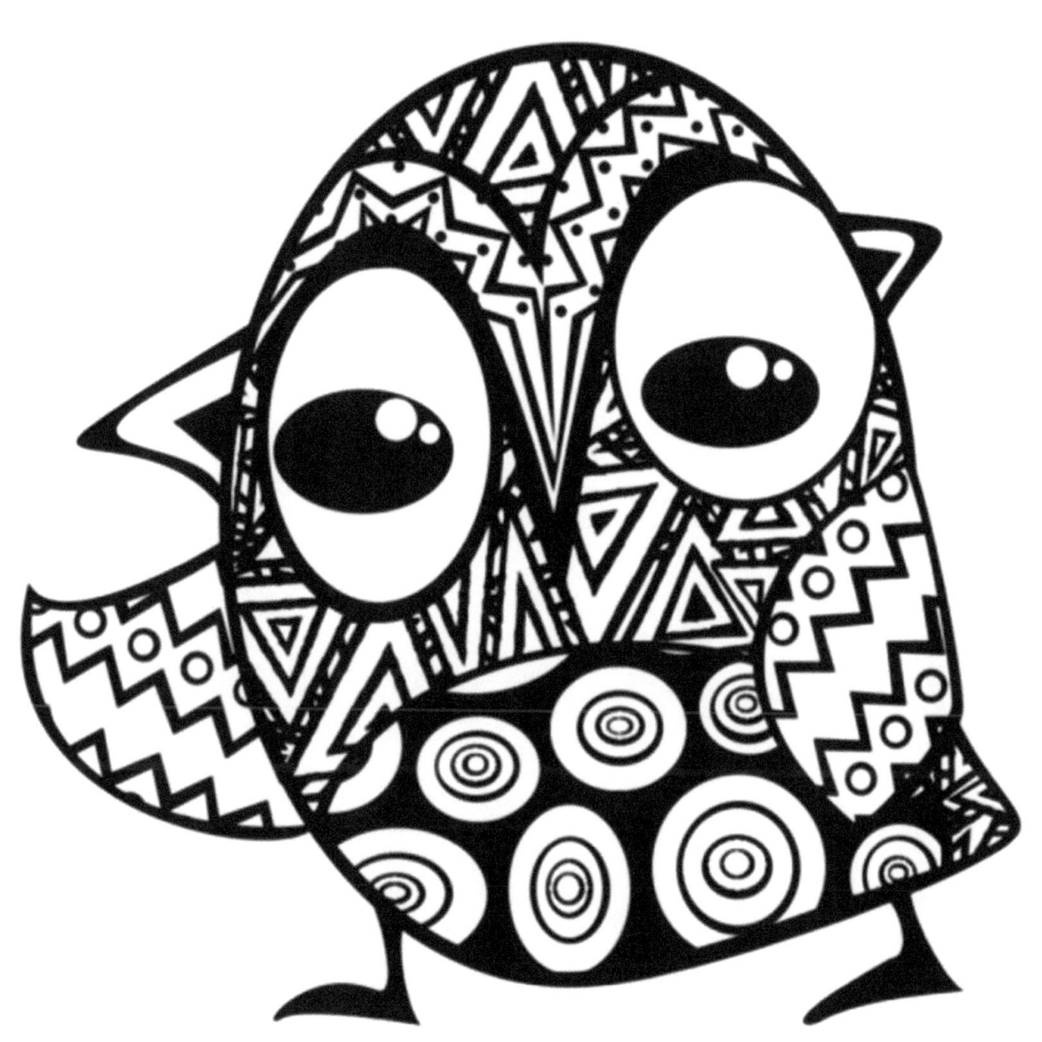

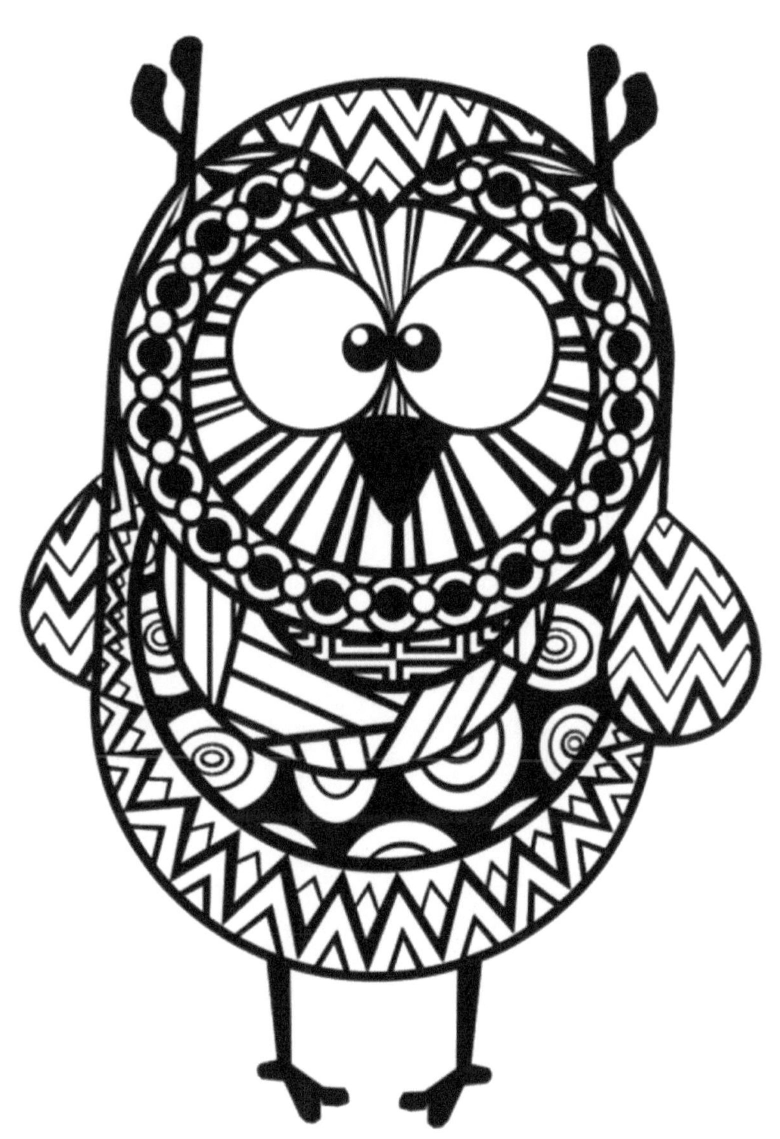

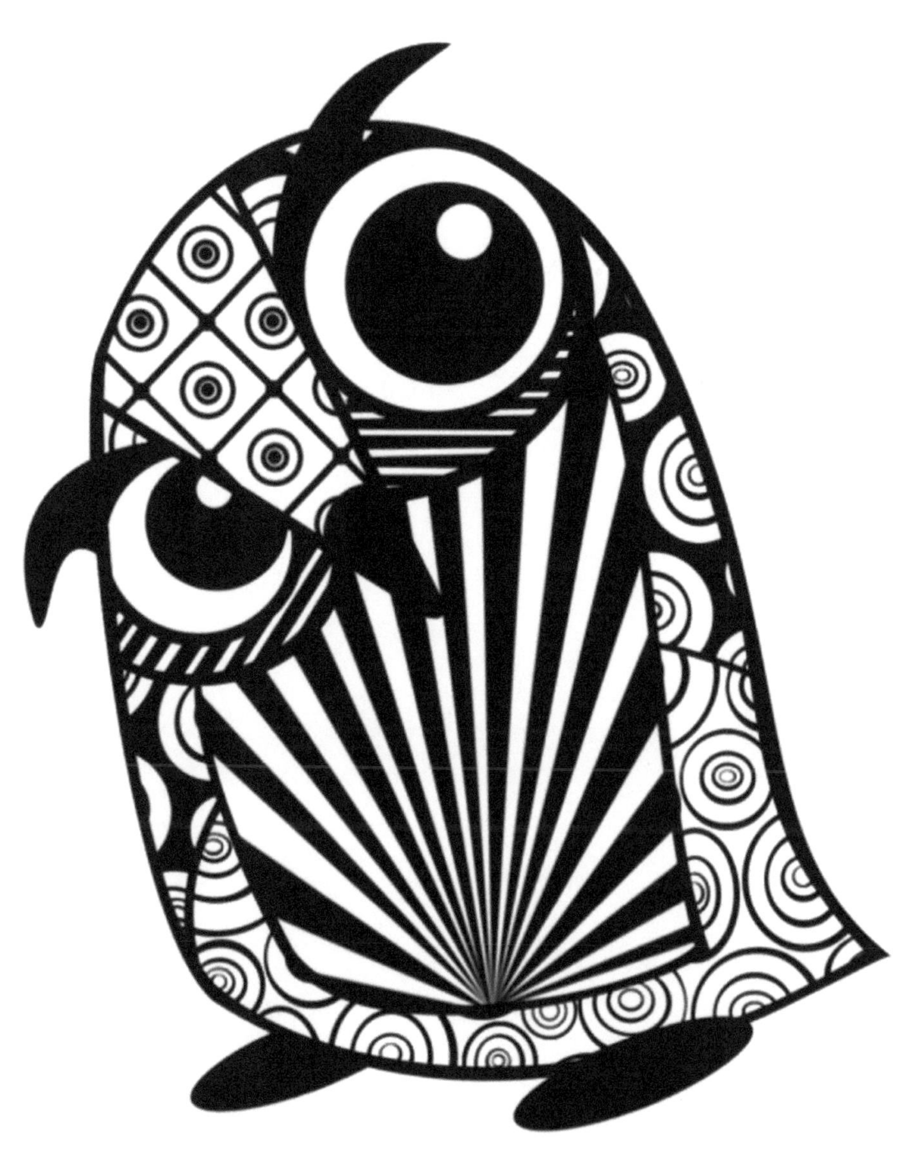

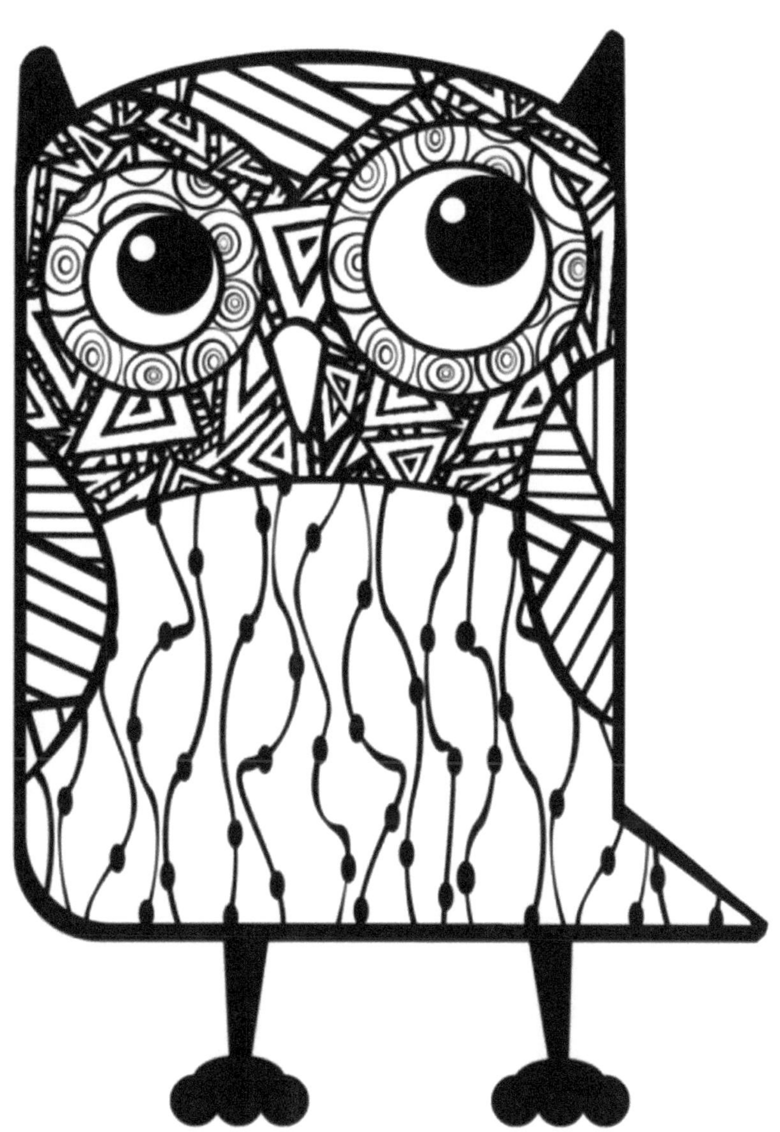

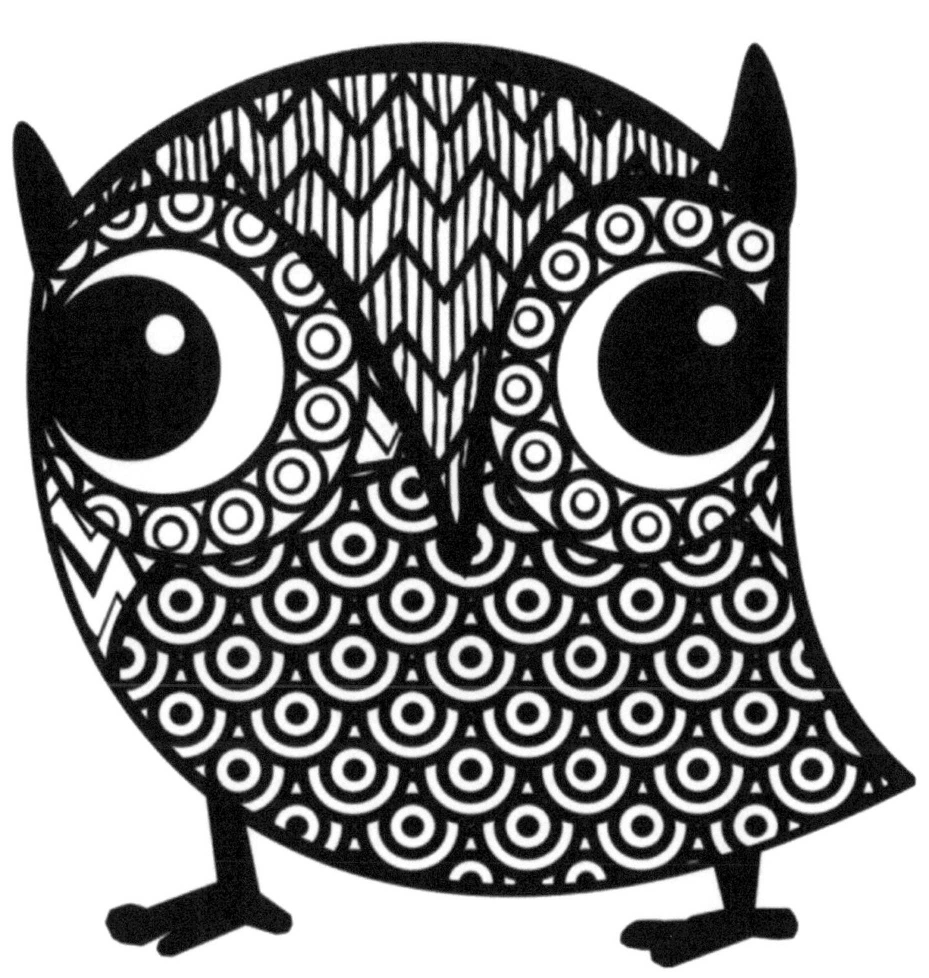